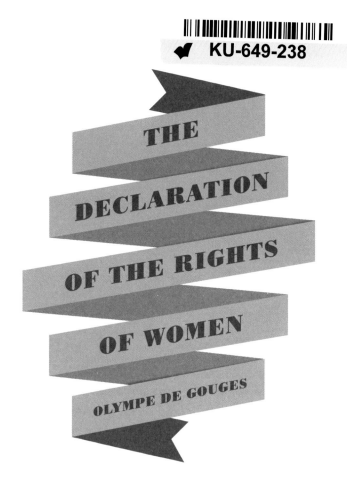

THE DECLARATION OF THE RIGHTS OF WOMEN

OLYMPE DE GOUGES

THE ORIGINAL MANIFESTO FOR JUSTICE, EQUALITY, & FREEDOM

THE DECLARATION OF THE RIGHTS OF WOMEN

OLYMPE DE GOUGES

Table of Contents

—

—

Amélie Falière—Sébastien Mourrain
Céline Gobinet—Éric Gosselet
Nathalie Ragondet—Paul Echegoyen
Daphné Hong—Carlos Felipe León
Sandrine Han Jin Kuang—Stéphane Kardos
Christophe Lautrette—Gérald Guerlais
Camille André—Lionel Richerand
Luc Desmarchelier—Hugues Mahoas
Yrgane Ramon—Louis Thomas
Maël Gourmelen—Maly Siri
Maïlys Vallade—Wassim Boutaleb J.
Marc Lizano et Carole Trébor—Sébastien Pelon
Jazzi—Aurélien Prédal
Aude Massot—Kness
Yasmine Gateau—Anne-Lise Boutin

Declaration of the Rights of Women and Female Citizens by Olympe de Gouges

INTRODUCTION

—

Just outside the center of Paris, in the densely populated district of Pantin, you can find the Place Olympe de Gouges. An undistinguished square, with a bakery and a couple of restaurants, it memorializes one of the French Revolution's most tragic victims: a woman whose bravery, in speaking out against the sexist and racist injustices of her time, gave a voice to millions—and whose most important work, published in 1789, remains relevant and resonant to this day.

Marie Gouze was born in 1748, some four hundred miles from Paris, in the southern town of Montauban. After a brief marriage ended by the death of her unloved husband, she moved in 1770 to Paris, where she embarked on a life in high society, started her literary career, and changed her name to the more impressive Olympe de Gouges. Her main concern, initially, was for the plight of the slaves of France's colonies: her play Zamore and Mirza, and several subsequent books and essays, established her as a tenacious advocate of emancipation.

Like many, de Gouges welcomed the French Revolution of 1789 and its upending of the existing political power structures; however, she rapidly perceived that revolutionary commitment to the rights of man did not extend to securing those same rights and freedoms for France's female citizens. In response to 1789's Declaration of the Rights of Man and of the Citizen, the central text of the Revolution, she published the Déclaration des droits de la Femme et de la Citoyenne, pointing out that, revolutionary as the earlier statement had been, it was only addressed to France's male citizens. A fair social order, and the true revolution, would not arrive until the state recognized women's rights, gave them a voice, and resolved domestic injustices such as a wife's inability to hold property, or an unmarried mother's lack of recourse to the law in matters of paternity.

As the Revolution of 1789 became the Terror of 1793, de Gouges paid the ultimate price for her outspoken calls for justice. She was beheaded in Paris in November 1793, a witness calling her "calm and serene" and saying that "such courage and beauty had never been seen before." Her revolutionary calls for sexual equality would not win out for over a century (women would not gain the vote in any European countries until the twentieth century, and in France not until 1944) but she is now recognized as one of the most courageous and influential of feminists, and her Déclaration retains its impressive power and relevance to this day.

Prelude

(Presented to the Legislative Assembly on October 28, 1791
and rejected by the Convention; published in the booklet
The Rights of Women addressed to Queen Marie Antoinette)

—

We mothers, daughters, and sisters, the female representatives of this nation, demand to be constituted into a national assembly.
Believing that ignorance, negligence, and scorn of the rights of women are the sole causes of public misfortune and of the corruption of governments, women have resolved to set forth in a solemn declaration, the natural, inalienable, and sacred rights of women, in order that this declaration, constantly present before all members of society, will serve as a perpetual reminder of their rights and duties; in order that the authoritative acts of women and the authoritative acts of men may, at any moment, be compared with the purposes of all political institutions and that these will thus be better fulfilled; and in order that citizens' demands, henceforth based on simple and incontestable principles, will always seek to uphold the constitution and good morals, for the happiness of all.

Consequently, the sex that is as superior in beauty as it is in courage during the sufferings of maternity, recognizes and declares in the presence and under the auspices of the Supreme Being, the following Rights of Women and of Female Citizens.

Illustrated by Gérald Guerlais

Article 1

Woman is born free and remains equal to man in her rights. Social distinctions should be based only on the common good.

Illustrated by Camille André

"Tremble, you trousered tyrants!
Women, our day has come:
Leave pity aside and trumpet
All the wrongs done by the bearded sex!
(*twice*)
For too long this has endured,
Our patience is at an end.
Rise Vesuvians, rise,
And wash clean the abuse of old.

Chorus
Liberty, shine your warmth
Bright upon our brows;
Tremble, tremble, jealous husbands,
Respect the petticoat brigade!
Tremble, tremble, jealous husbands,
Respect the petticoat brigade!

Man, this savage despot,
Was quick to proclaim his rights;
Now let us create rights that befit us,
Now let us have laws that befit us! (*twice*)
Man in seventeen ninety-three,
Cared for no one but himself,
Let us today think of ourselves,
And create our own 'Marseillaise'!"
—
Louise de Chaumont, *La Marseillaise des cotillons*, song published in the first issue of *La République des femmes, journal des cotillons*, June 1848.

"I myself have never been able to find out precisely what feminism is: I only know that people call me a feminist whenever I express sentiments that differentiate me from a doormat."
—
Rebecca West (1892–1983).

12

"For too long, women have been left hoping for a social condition equal to that of men. When, in 1789, Olympe de Gouges presented her list of grievances and demands to the General Assembly on behalf of women, she was told that it was pointless to examine the condition of woman since a complete change was about to take place in society and women would be liberated from men. The revolution broke out: the rights of man were proclaimed but women remained in servitude. The women who had worked for the Revolution naively believed that they had won their share of liberty. When they found themselves utterly disregarded, they protested. And then they were ridiculed, scorned, and insulted, and, later, when they went to demand their rights from the Commune Council, [they were] driven away ignominiously by revolutionary politician Chaumette. These outraged women protested; they formed a club to defend not only their own specific rights but the common interests of all. The Convention, the Great Convention, closed down their organization and voted to ban women from assembling to engage in public affairs. And, at the same time that these autocratic revolutionaries were decreeing inequality, they made certain that the terms Equality and Liberty resounded in every corner of the world! [...] Women of France, as I stand here before you, I say to you that those who deny us equality today will deny us equality in the future. Let us then look to ourselves; let us not abandon our demands. For centuries we have too often been the victims of bad faith to forget ourselves now and believe that by working for the well-being of all we shall have our share of that general good. (*Applause*)."

—

Hubertine Auclert, speech given to the third Socialist Worker Congress, Marseille, October 22, 1879.

Article 2

The purpose of any political association is the preservation of the natural and imprescriptible rights of woman and man; these rights are liberty, property, security, and, above all, resistance to oppression.

Illustrated by Lionel Richerand

"No environment, no territory, no generation is spared the violence done to women. Everywhere inequality and domination are perpetuated by it."

—

Marisol Touraine, press release, International Day for the Elimination of Violence against Women, November 25, 2015.

"Imagine with John Lennon a world with no religion. Imagine no suicide bombers, no 9/11, no 7/7, no Crusades, no witch-hunts, no Gunpowder Plot, no Indian partition, no Israeli/Palestinian wars, no Serb/Croat/Muslim massacres, no persecution of Jews as 'Christ killers,' no Northern Ireland 'troubles,' no 'honor killings,' no shiny-suited bouffant-haired televangelists fleecing gullible people of their money. Imagine no Taliban to blow up ancient statues, no public beheadings of blasphemers, no flogging of female skin for the crime of showing an inch of it."

—

Richard Dawkins, *The God Delusion*, 2006.

"The three monotheistic religions—and I mean all three—fundamentally profess the same detestation of women, of desire, urges, passions, and sensuality, and of liberty— all liberties. So let's not get worked up about the relevance or not of teaching religion in school; the real urgency is to teach atheism."

—
Michel Onfray, *Traité d'athéologie*, 2005.

"God to the rescue to make sure the difference between the sexes holds firm—this God that misogynists always put on their side…"

—
Benoîte Groult, *Le Féminisme au masculin*, 1980.

"Among peoples who are truly free, women are free and are adored."

—
Louis Antoine de Saint-Just, *L'Esprit de la Révolution et de la Constitution de France*, part III, chap. XII, "Des femmes," 1791.

Article 3

The principle of all sovereignty lies essentially in the Nation, which is but the union of Woman and Man; no body, no individual should exercise authority that does not derive expressly from it.

Illustrated by Luc Desmarchelier

"The notion of freedom of movement is key. In the nineteenth century, cities were sexually discriminatory places where most women were unable to move about freely. Those who did so were streetwalkers. A woman needed a mask to penetrate the space appropriated by men, to switch from the status of observed to that of observer. George Sand was one of the exceptions to the rule that only men could saunter about the streets. To saunter and observe, to gorge yourself on humanity, you have to walk—a lot and for a long time. Everything about fashion conspired against such freedom: dresses, hats, shoes all condemned women to immobility."

—

Christine Bard, *Une histoire politique du pantalon*, 2010.

"Who speaks in those wise weighty tomes in libraries? Who speaks in the Capitol? Who speaks in the temple? Who speaks from the rostrum and who speaks in our laws? It is men who have the floor. The world is what men say it is. And the words of men appear to be at odds. To make us forget this they all say the same thing: 'what men say is what is.' Men's words make the world."

—

Annie Leclerc, *Parole de femme*, 1974.

"I had my first meeting last week at Choisy-le-Roi. The first evening I was a bit panicky; I didn't say much; I was with a man, I let him speak. The second evening I began speaking. The third evening was ok; someone asked me a question and as I was about to answer, he cut in. I heard some women in the room saying: "Isn't he going to let her speak? Let the woman speak!" Then he shut up. After that, I really felt that I needed to speak because the women were waiting for me to speak, and I spoke a lot more freely."

—

A female worker from the Lip watch factory in Besançon, "Lip au féminin," *Les Pétroleuses*, no. 0, 1974.

"We need to cure ourselves of being women. Not of being born women but of being brought up as women in a man's world, of going through each stage and each act of our lives with men's eyes and with men's criteria. And we'll never bring about this cure by continuing to listen to what these men have to say in our name or for our good."

—

Benoîte Groult, *Ainsi soit-elle*, 1975.

Article 4

Liberty and justice consist in restoring to others all that belongs to them; hence, the only limits to the exercise of the natural rights of woman are found in the perpetual male tyranny opposed to them; these limits must be reformed according to the laws of nature and reason.

Illustrated by Hugues Mahoas

"Roxanne to Usbek, in Paris.

Yes, I have deceived you; I have seduced your eunuchs; I have made sport of your jealousy; and I have managed to turn your frightful seraglio into a place of pleasure and delight.

I shall soon die; the poison will course through my veins.

What else should I do here since the only man who kept me alive is no more?

I am dying but my spirit will not take flight alone: I have dispatched before me those sacrilegious guardians who spilt the finest blood in the world.

How could you have imagined me to be so gullible as to think that my only purpose in this world was to delight in your every whim? That while you allowed yourself every liberty, you should have the right to thwart all my desires?

No—I may have lived in servitude but I have always been free: I have refashioned your laws according to those of nature and my spirit has always remained independent.

You should thank me then for the sacrifice I made you; for having sunk so low as to appear faithful to you; for, like a coward, hiding in my heart what I should have made public to the world; for having profaned virtue itself by allowing my submission to your fantasies to be called by that name.

You were amazed never to find in me the transports of love. If you had truly known me you would have found all the violence of hate.

But for so long you have had the satisfaction of believing that this heart of mine was yours alone. We were both happy: you believed me to be deceived and I was deceiving you.

My language no doubt surprises you. Could it be possible that after overwhelming you with pain I might even force you to admire my courage? But it is too late now: the poison consumes me; my strength leaves me; the pen falls from my hand; even my hate grows weaker; death takes me.

From the Seraglio at Ispahan, the 8th of the Moon of Rebiab 1, 1720."

—

Montesquieu, *Lettres persanes, letter* CLXI, 1721.

"The female sex has been so vilified in Europe that women no longer even think to demand what is theirs by right. If the law had guaranteed women the right to exercise love in freedom, we would have seen less pretence of love—the target of our unjust sarcasm—and we would have the freedom to divorce, without the slightest inconvenience. The subjection of women is in no way to man's advantage. How deluded is the male sex by our wearing a chain that it finds hateful; how such a bond makes man suffer for having reduced woman to slavery!

In more general terms, social progress depends upon women's progress toward freedom, and social decadence corresponds to a decline in women's freedom. Thus, extending the rights of women is the fundamental prerequisite of all social progress."
—
Charles Fourier, *Vers la liberté en amour*, 1817–1819.

"We cannot act as though colonialism never took place or deny the existence of racial representations. Similarly with gender, we cannot ignore the sedimentation of sexual norms. Indeed, the world needs norms to function, but we are free to search for those norms that suit us best."
—
Judith Butler, Interviewed by Eric Aeschimann for *Le Nouvel Observateur*, 2013.

Article 5

The laws of nature and reason prohibit all acts that are injurious to society; no hindrance should be placed on anything that is not prohibited by these wise and divine laws, nor should anyone be constrained to do anything other than they require.

Illustrated by Yrgane Ramon

"Women are dominated not because they are sexually women, not because they have a different anatomy, not because they might naturally have different ways of thinking and acting than men, not because they might be fragile or incapable, but because they have the privilege of fertility and of being able to reproduce males. Contraception liberates them from the very place where they were held captive. In fact it is quite remarkable to see how vitally important contraception is for women in all societies. Recently, sociologists conducted a public opinion survey to find out what was the most significant event of our century. The majority of men responded that it was the conquest of space. For 90% of women, contraception came top of the list.

Women's access to contraception represents a genuine turning point in human history. True, over the centuries women's status has varied. But despite these variations, the representation of women has always remained at a level determined by male domination in the classic sense of the term: women represent the home and must confine themselves to control of their biological function. For this common substrate to change radically, women must attain the legal status of autonomous individuals. So, as I see it, contraception is the key lever to female emancipation."

—

Françoise Héritier, *Masculin/Féminin II. Dissoudre la hiérarchie*, 2008.

"A woman a hundred years ago knew her life would be over the moment she got herself pregnant."
—
Rachel Cusk, *Arlington Park*, 2006.

"The revival of naturalism, reinstating the worn-out concept of maternal instinct and lauding female masochism and sacrifice, constitutes the greatest threat to female emancipation and gender equality."
—
Élisabeth Badinter, *Le Conflit. La femme et la mère*, 2010.

"The relationship between parents and children, like that between spouses, should be freely chosen. It is not even true that for a woman a child is a privileged accomplishment; people are quick to say that a woman is coquettish or amorous or lesbian or ambitious as a result of being childless; her sexual life, her goals, and the values she pursues are deemed to be child substitutes. In fact, it is unclear what is the cause and what is the effect: one might just as well say that lacking love or an occupation, or being unable to satisfy her homosexual tendencies is what makes a woman want to have a child. This pseudo-naturalism conceals a social and artificial morality. The idea that a child is the ultimate goal of woman is barely worthy of an advertising slogan. It leads directly to a second preconception that a child is sure to find happiness in its mother's arms. There is no such thing as an 'unnatural' mother because there is nothing natural about maternal love—but for the very same reason, there are bad mothers."
—
Simone de Beauvoir, *The Second Sex*, 1949.

29

Article 6

The law should be the expression of the general will; all citizens, female and male, should participate in person or through their representatives in its formation; it should be the same for all: female and male citizens, being equal in the eyes of the law, should be equally eligible for all public positions of rank, offices, and employment according to their ability and with no other distinction than those of their virtue and their talent.

Illustrated by Louis Thomas

"Reminding women that gallantry is a political insult, the parties, like English clubs, resist change and desperately replicate a warlike corporatism. Those women who, willing to serve an ideal of social transformation, wish to enter politics are rejected by these partisan structures whose language serves as a sharp stick."
—
Yvette Roudy, "La parité domestiquée," *Le Monde*, September 5, 2004.

"Don't become women who do good works; don't doze off in women's clubs. Don't forget to take feminism to where it belongs: the political arena."
—
Marguerite Durand (1864–1936).

"Contrary to what it would be comforting to believe, the female condition is not improving. Not across the world, as we know, nor even in France. After thirty years of female victories, male hegemony in Europe is still striking. To refuse to see this, to agree to shut your mother's feminism away in the attic is to risk seeing woman's hard-won place in society stagnate or, worse still, decline."

—

Benoîte Groult, *Ainsi soit-elle*, 1975.

"Colette's thinking is guided neither by the imperative of the reproduction of the species, nor by the imperative of social stability assured by the couple and the assurances they make. The only constant is her concern with the freeing of the subject 'woman,' who wishes to attain sensual freedom in order to maintain her curiosity and her creativity, not as part of a couple but in a plurality of connections."

—

Julia Kristeva, *Colette. Un génie féminin*, 2007.

Article 7

No woman is exempt;
she is accused,
arrested, and detained
in cases determined
by law. Women,
like men, obey
this rigorous law.

Illustrated by Maël Gourmelen

"When the dictionary has been revised and the language feminized, each of its words will be an expressive call to order for male egoism."

—

Hubertine Auclert (1848–1914).

"Yes, indeed, gentlemen—you who are such authorities on the internal workings of the soul and the psyche—reading does give women ideas. What sacrilege! How then are we to stem the flow of pleasure that reading brings to women?"

—

Laure Adler and Stefan Bollmann,
Les femmes qui lisent sont dangereuses, 2006.

" 'What has suddenly got into women? They've all starting writing books. What have they got to say that's so important?' a weekly paper recently asked—though it had never questioned why men had been writing for two thousand years and what they might possibly have left to say!"

—

Benoite Groult, *Ainsi soit-elle*, 1975.

"These poets will exist! And when the infinite servitude of woman is broken, when she lives for herself and through herself—and man, hitherto abominable, has given her her freedom—she too will be a poet! Woman will discover the unknown! Will her worlds of ideas be different from ours? She will find strange, unfathomable, repulsive, and delicious things; we shall take these and we shall understand them."

—
Arthur Rimbaud, letter to Paul Demeny, Charleville, May 15, 1871.

"We should be very wrong to plagiarize men, to follow their example, and to walk blindly along the paths they take. We have in ourselves a precious raw material: our ignorance. We must beware of losing this asset by filling our minds with the same old clutter that men have accumulated in theirs for centuries."

—
Alexandra David-Néel, "Les femmes et la question sociale," *La Fronde*, May 28, 1902.

The law must establish only such penalties as are strictly and obviously necessary and no one should be punished except by virtue of a law established and enacted prior to the offense and legally applied to women.

Illustrated by Maly Siri

"Early solitary desire is one of the rare memories that can remind women that we are fully sexual before 'beauty' comes into the picture, and can be so after and beyond the beauty myth; and that sexual feeling does not have to depend on being looked at.
Men take this core for granted in themselves: We see that, sanctioned by the culture, men's sexuality simply is. They do not have to earn it with their appearance. We see that men's desire precedes contact with women. It does not lie dormant waiting to spring into being only in response to a woman's will."
—
Naomi Wolf, *The Beauty Myth: How Images of Beauty are used Against Women*, 1990.

"In our society, such as it is made, with this form of sale that we call a dowry and this tyrant that we call a husband, adultery is nothing other than a protest in support of that primary and most sacred of liberties, the liberty to love, and against the enslavement of woman and the despotism of marriage—an anarchic but legitimate protest; violent, unpredictable, but as profound and unquenchable as nature itself."
—
Victor Hugo, *Choses vues*, Guernsey, 1860.

40

"The very essence of marriage, as established in our morality, is to unite a virgin girl with an already experienced man, and to entrust to the knowledge of the man the education of the girl. This system is founded upon the principle or, in my opinion, the preconception of female virginity. But even if we agree that girls should come to marriage in this state of purity and ignorance, it is still vital that these novices should find themselves with good teachers and that their preparation for marriage be placed in safe hands. The present system prohibits girls from acquiring even a theoretical knowledge of love before marriage. And it also, indirectly, prevents the majority of men from acquiring, in a suitable manner, the very experience that one of the spouses needs to possess. If, during the period of freedom prior to marriage, young men are forced to seek instruction from prostitutes, is this in fact a free choice, a preference on their part? On the contrary, would they not prefer to find this mistress—whom, at present, they must seek at random—nearer to hand, among their close acquaintances? Instead of squandering the ardor of their youth in brief and furtive encounters, would they not prefer to give it fully to a female friend who is their equal; whom a shared tenderness had similarly prepared for the knowledge and exchange of desire? […] Under the severest of penalties, you prohibit young women from coming to marriage already instructed in love, but in so doing you also handicap their future teachers. This is to commit too many errors at once."
—
Léon Blum, *Du mariage*, 1907.

41

Article 9

Once any woman is found guilty, the full rigor of the law applies.

Illustrated by Maïlys Vallade

"I should like, first of all, to share with you my conviction as a woman—I apologize for doing so before this Assembly almost entirely composed of men: No woman resorts to abortion with a light heart. You have only to listen to women. It is always an ordeal and it will always be an ordeal.

[...] But we can no longer close our eyes to the three hundred thousand abortions that, each year, maim the women of this country, that flout our laws, and that humiliate and traumatize those who resort to them.

History shows us that the great debates that have briefly divided the French people appear, with the passing of time, as a necessary stage in the formation of a new social consensus that becomes part of our country's tradition of tolerance and reason."

—

Simone Veil, Statement of reasons for the reform of abortion legislation, speech made before the French National Assembly, November 26, 1974.

"Their very frequency makes these crises of pregnancy virtually commonplace. One woman, to avoid disgrace, commits suicide; another kills her child; another—a young worker, maid, farm girl— driven away by her boss, falls into prostitution. Thanks to abortion, these terrible outcomes are becoming less common; when the law ceases to make abortion a crime and recognizes a woman's right not to be a mother except by choice, abortion will cease."

—

Madeleine Pelletier, *L'Émancipation sexuelle de la femme*, 1911.

"Ladies and Gentlemen, you have been told of the need and the advantages of paternity searches. […] However, when I think of all those women for whom the father of their child will remain elusive, of all those who will shrink from the formalities, the red tape, of all those, particularly, whose dignity will not allow them to ask of or owe anything to the wretched man who has repudiated them… I tell myself that we would be wrong to see these paternity searches as anything other than a first step, a very timid one at that, and one that must be followed by many more on the steep, obstacle-strewn path along which women, like slaves, drag themselves wearisomely toward full justice and complete freedom. I tell myself that it is less important to give a betrayed mother and an abandoned child the opportunity to seek out and punish the deceitful lover, the unworthy father, than to put them both in a position to manage without him, to ignore him as he ignores them, and to shun him as he has scorned them.

In fact, the great problem that occupies us today may have another solution. That of opening every door to woman, revealing to her every horizon; making her mistress of her own destiny, capable of living her own life, of making her own place in the sun; abolishing too the odious morality that heaps reproach on the sacred brow of mothers when they have allowed themselves to become such outside the rites of law; and then—and here is the key—creating this 'Maternity Fund,' achieving the assimilation of maternal function and social function which, alone, can guarantee mothers both independence and security… this is the great, the true remedy to so many of the evils that afflict us."
—
Nelly Roussel, speech given at the demonstration in support of paternity searches, February 9, 1910.

Article 10

No one should be hounded
for their opinions,
however radical;
woman has the right
to mount the scaffold
so she should equally have
the right to mount the
rostrum, provided
that her actions do not
disturb public order as
established by law.

Illustrated by Wassim Boutaleb J.

"For Man—who is a social individual—to advance, to ascend, for Humanity to progress, Woman—who is the creator of children—must also advance, progress, ascend, and grow. But one does not grow in servitude; one does not climb, one does not ascend when one remains in voluntary subjection. Human beings progress only through the development of their consciousness and in the pursuit and practice of liberty.

In his day, Socrates told Man: 'Know yourself.' The time has come to say to Woman: 'Own yourself.' Belonging to oneself is not only a right, it is a duty. Woman who is subject to Man, Woman as vassal of Man, causes Man himself to stoop, to diminish. The tyranny of the one has as its corollary the degradation of the other—in other words, the debasement of all.

Whosoever enslaves, enslaves himself: all despots place themselves in chains. […] There is an innate solidarity between Man and Woman; a fatal, indomitable solidarity between the liberty of Woman and the progress of Civilization."

—
Léon Richer, *La Femme libre*, 1877.

"Wherever we are—at home, at work, in a revolutionary group—we get hassle. It seems that it's only when we're serious about things that we get anything done. We've had enough of guys and their masochism. Power to women—they're the least likely to be serious! My body isn't just a way of carrying my head around because I wouldn't know how to hold it up otherwise. As soon as I put on a guy's head, an intellectual head, or even my father's head, it was easier to get things done. A chick who isn't a chick doesn't have the right to exist, she's not fuckable. But a word to the wise. Those guys who say that a chick who speaks and writes isn't fuckable, those guys are in revolutionary groups and they're running them. So, if I want a revolution that allows me to have a body, to laugh and stick with my own head, I'll just have to make it myself somewhere else."
—
"Pourquoi je suis au mouvement de libération des femmes," *L'Idiot Liberté, Le torchon brûle!*, no. 0, December 1970.

"No, the war between the sexes was not born out of feminism; on the contrary, it must end with it. Men, if only you knew how much happier you will be when women are happier!"
—
Nelly Roussel, 1909.

49

Article 11

Free communication of thought and opinions is one of the most precious rights of woman, as this liberty ensures that children are recognized by their father. Every female citizen may therefore say freely, I am the mother of a child who belongs to you; no barbarous prejudice should force her to conceal the truth—provided responsibility is accepted for any abuse of this liberty in cases determined by law.

Illustrated by Marc Lizano and Carole Trébor

"Such material difficulties were formidable; but much worse were the immaterial. The indifference of the world which Keats and Flaubert and other men of genius have found so hard was in her case not indifference but hostility. The world did not say to her as it did to them, Write if you choose; it makes no difference to me. The world said with a guffaw, Write? What's the good of your writing?"

—
Virginia Woolf, *A Room of One's Own*, 1929.

"In twenty-five centuries of philosophy, women have been regarded as the objects of thinking and certainly not as subjects who think. They are either appearance (there to be seen) or symbol. […] And today the issue facing women is not only one of identity and difference, but one of subject and object. To become subjects… is a constant struggle—not only political or civil subjects, but also subjects in thought."

—
Geneviève Fraisse, *La Fabrique du féminisme. Textes et entretiens*, 2012.

"From the moment they see reading as a way of swapping the narrowness of domestic life for the boundless space of thought, of imagination, but also of knowledge, women become dangerous. In reading, they appropriate knowledge and experience for which they have not been predestined by society."
—
Laure Adler and Stefan Bollmann,
Les femmes qui lisent sont dangereuses,
2006.

"Make the doors upon a woman's wit and it will out the casement; shut that and 'twill out at the key-hole; stop that, 'twill fly with the smoke out at the chimney."
—
William Shakespeare, *As You Like It*, 1599.

Article 12

Guaranteeing the rights of woman and the female citizen requires the existence of a greater good; this guarantee must be instituted for the advantage of all, and not for the private benefit of those on whom it is conferred.

Illustrated by Sébastien Pelon

"How many men choose to cultivate this half-witted attitude to household chores to appease their partner? It's a real talent. This avoidance behavior is absolutely classic and can be commonly seen in children who balk at doing some chore or other.

The latest men's magazines even encourage this don't-know-how-to behavior by men. For example, in November 2000, the first issue of the magazine *Maximal* told its readers 'how to get out of doing housework.' How? By adopting a paradoxical approach, i.e. cleaning without really cleaning. The magazine advised readers to go the extra mile to show good will but to 'vacuum at Formula 1 speed' or to 'leave smears on the glasses' when washing up. This handy advice will—the inspired journalist continues—allow you to gain 'a reputation as helpful, considerate, and domesticated without ever needing to get your hands dirty.'

Apparently even more surprising is that men find a significant ally in the innate female guilt that is immediately triggered. From early childhood, without our even realizing it, dolls, saucepan sets, irons, and ironing boards have shaped girls, Christmas after Christmas, into housewives. Our family upbringing, steeped in age-old sociocultural traditions, is there to underpin the idea that women should master the domestic arts. So we find that girls help out at home infinitely more often than their brothers. And the advertising-led media strike a final blow in support of one gender taking responsibility for housework. The glaring inequality that lies nestled under the dust, between the dishes, at the very heart of the home, is anything but a cause for celebration. These household chores, about which we talk so little but which reveal so much—perhaps everything—about the relationship between the sexes, are very quick to expose the gulf between female know-how and male don't-know-how-to. Housework represents a global no-man's-land: it relates neither to wage-earning nor to male territory."

Clémentine Autain, *Alter égaux. Invitation au féminisme*, 2001.

"Women have always had the unfortunate gift of translating their most ardent love into domestic work. Dusting, washing up, vacuuming, these are ways of proving your love. Though it was often hard to devote such a large part of my free time to what Proust called these 'arts of nothingness,' especially at a time when the term job-sharing hadn't even been invented, I got through it by raising each chore to the rank of a demonstration of love. Apparently, it was the future George Sand who, of the two of us, was the first to suspect that women were on to a loser here."
—
Benoîte Groult, *Histoire d'une évasion*, 1997.

"For all of you, woman is merchandise that can be bought, the cheapest with money, others with songs and promises, and assurances, and a long wait. But in the end there's no real difference."
—
Zoé Oldenbourg, *The Cornerstone*, 1953.

"There are men who are happier as gatherers, with interior decorating, and taking children to the park and women who are built to spear mammoth, shout, and set traps."
—
Virginie Despentes, *King Kong Théorie*, 2007.

Article 13

The contributions of women and men to the maintenance of public authority and to administrative costs are equal. Women share in all the drudgery, in all the painful tasks; therefore, they must have the same share in the distribution of posts, employment, offices, rewards, and responsibilities.

Illustrated by Jazzi

"This ideal of a woman who is white and attractive but not a whore, well married but not retiring, who works but is not so successful that she outshines her husband, slim but not neurotic about food, who remains forever young without being disfigured by cosmetic surgery, a glowing mother but not swamped by nappies and homework, a good hostess but not a traditional housewife, cultivated but less so than a man, this fortunate white woman who is constantly being brandished under our nose, this woman we should all make the effort to be like, apart from the fact that she seems to have to go to a lot of trouble to achieve very little… I, at least, have never come across her anywhere. In fact, I'm sure she doesn't exist."

—

Virginie Despentes, *King Kong Théorie*, 2006.

"We are far more like men than we are like this factitious creature, this conventional being they have always wanted us to be. It is men who, through their inculcation, through the particular morality they have foisted upon us, through their literature, through their brutality and their demands, have created a woman both monstrous and ideal, a type from which we have still not dared to deviate […]. We have had to conceal our humanity beneath a conventional femininity that they invented for their own advantage."

—

Jeanne Loiseau, aka Daniel-Lesueur, in *La Fronde*, 1900.

"Even more than the beautiful images, the omnipresence of unattainable models encloses many women in self-hatred, in a wasteful and destructive spiral on which they expend an exorbitant amount of energy. The obsession with being slim betrays a persistent condemnation of all that is female, a feeling of dark and devastating guilt. The fear of rejection gives rise to ideas of using surgery to reshape a body perceived as inert, disenchanted matter that is as malleable as we see fit, an external object with which the self does not identify in any way. And the globalization of the cosmetic industry and media groups is leading to the spread across our entire planet of a single model of whiteness, sometimes reactivating iniquitous local hierarchies."
—
Mona Chollet, *Beauté fatale. Les nouveaux visages d'une aliénation féminine*, 2012.

"One is not born a woman; one becomes a woman. No biological, psychic, or economic destiny defines the form that the human female adopts within society; it is civilization as a whole that fabricates this intermediary product between the male and the eunuch that is known as the female. Only the mediation of another can constitute an individual as an *Other*. If they existed in isolation, children would not be able to see themselves as sexually differentiated."
—
Simone de Beauvoir, *The Second Sex*, 1949.

Article 14

Female and male citizens
have the right to have
demonstrated to them,
or to their representatives,
the need for public taxes.
Women should agree to these
only on condition that they
be entitled to an equal share,
not only in wealth, but also in
public administration and in
determining the proportion,
assessment base, collection,
and duration of such taxes.

Illustrated by Aurélien Prédal

"Doubt and fear are women's worst enemies. Doubt shackles their ankles and fear invades their mind. They doubt for fear of being slandered and with this dagger of doubt they slash themselves to pieces and become white with fear. This female pallor is much admired; a thousand explanations are given for it and it is found endlessly attractive. Women, free yourselves from the lacerations of fear, stand up, straight and proud, not like clinging, dependent creepers but like tall trees with solid roots! A lone woman can grow, spread, and create an entire forest."

—

Taslima Nasreen, *Femmes, manifestez-vous!*, 1991.

"The narrowness of the existing concept of woman's independence and her emancipation; the fear of loving a man who is not her social equal; the fear that love will rob her of her freedom and independence; the horror that love or the joy of motherhood will only hamper her in the exercise of her profession—all these together make of the emancipated modern woman a compulsory vestal, before whom life, with its great purifying sorrows and its deep and captivating joys, rolls by, leaving her soul untouched, ungripped."

—

Emma Goldman, lecture published in *Mother Earth*, no. 1, March 1906, reprinted in *The Tragedy of Woman's Emancipation*, 1906.

"Today, every woman must be both a man and a woman. No one can be two human beings at once. So why demand this of women? We have met women caught in this trap, all admirable in their courage, in their desire to escape it, their perseverance, their generosity. Unaffected women who question themselves, women who are reluctant to give in. Today, the female condition is no longer defined by submission and power relations, but by the invisible corset that each woman wears under her skin. These days she has to fight for her survival, she has to fight to be herself, at every stage in her life; she has to fight against herself and against society in order to break out of this invisible corset.

The feminist no longer exists. The woman of today has gone beyond the fight against man. She needs man. Even the seemingly strongest women have confided this to us: they give the impression of being fully in control but they need man.

Woman's situation can change: not through warlike acts but through a revolution—which she and man must carry out together. No, this time it will not be enough to burn our bras. We need society to become engaged in undoing this invisible corset. In order to liberate woman, the whole of society must be liberated—and that includes man."

—

Éliette Abécassis and Caroline Bongrand, *Le Corset invisible*, 2007.

Article 15

Women as a body, joining together with men as a body in paying taxes, have the right to hold any public agent accountable for their actions.

Illustrated by Aude Massot

"For millennia, men have slit each other's throats for causes just and unjust: but the causes arose from them alone; never has the threat of death come from those who care for the wounded and rebuild the generations."

—

Marcelle Tinayre, *La Veillée des armes*, 1915.

"To call woman the weaker sex is a libel; it is man's injustice to women. […] If non-violence is the law of our being, the future is with woman."

—

Mahatma Gandhi, *All Men Are Brothers*, 1942–1956.

"The future of man
is woman
She is the color of his soul
She is his murmur
and his noise
And without her he is
nothing but blasphemy
He is but a stone
without the fruit
From his mouth blows
a wild wind
His life belongs to mayhem
And his own hand destroys
him.

I tell you that man
is born for woman
and born for love
All that is of the ancient world
will change
First life and then death
And all things will be shared
White bread, kisses
that bleed
We shall see the couple
and their reign
snowing like orange blossom."
—
Louis Aragon, *Le Fou d'Elsa*, 1963.

"Dismissing then those pretty
feminine phrases, which the
men condescendingly use to
soften our slavish dependence,
and despising that weak
elegancy of mind, exquisite
sensibility, and sweet docility
of manners, supposed to be
the sexual characteristics of
the weaker vessel, I wish to
show that elegance is inferior
to virtue, that the first object of
laudable ambition is to obtain
a character as a human being,
regardless of the distinction of
sex; and that secondary views
should be brought to
this simple touchstone."
—
Mary Wollstonecraft, *A Vindication of the Rights of Woman*, 1792.

Article 16

Any society that is
without guaranteed
rights and separation
of powers, is without
a constitution; a constitution
is void if the majority
of individuals comprising
the nation has not
cooperated in its drafting.

Illustrated by Kness

"[…] for woman, there is from the start a conflict between her autonomous existence and her 'otherness;' she is taught that in order to please, she must seek to please, she must make herself an object; therefore she must renounce her autonomy. She is treated like a living doll and freedom is denied her; and so, a vicious circle is formed, for the less she exercises her freedom to understand, grasp, and discover the world around her, the less she will discover its resources, the less she will dare to affirm herself as a subject; yet if she were encouraged in this, she would be capable of demonstrating the same lively exuberance, the same curiosity, the same spirit of initiative, and the same boldness as a boy."
—
Simone de Beauvoir, *The Second Sex*, 1949.

"Only a man could launch the idea that the happiness of a woman should consist in serving and pleasing a man."
—
Margaret Fuller, *Woman in the Nineteenth Century*, 1843.

"A woman is authentic when she resembles the image of herself she has seen in her dreams."
—
Pedro Almodóvar (1949-).

"The veil is far from being a simple religious sign, like the crucifix that girls and boys might wear around their neck. The veil—the *hijab*—is not a simple scarf worn around the head; it must conceal the body entirely. Above all, the veil abolishes the gender mix in society and materializes the radical and draconian separation of female space and male space; more precisely, it defines and limits female space. The *hijab* is an utterly barbaric Islamic dogma written on the female body and taking control of it."
—
Chahdortt Djavann, *Bas les voiles!*, 2003.

"Domestic harpies or Messalinas, holy women or whores, devoted mothers or unworthy mothers. Okay, these types are codified and accepted and we continue to play our roles. Yet the fact that we should try to re-imagine each act of our lives from our own perspective, to question everything from suffering the 'In pain shall you bring forth children' for so long as an expression of divine will, to the humble and passive scenario of happiness dreamt up for us by Freud, our 'Little Father,' this is deemed indecent and unacceptable. Men have always been delighted to find us unpredictable, coquettish, jealous, possessive, venal, frivolous… admirable failings they have carefully encouraged because they find them reassuring. But what if these creatures should start to think and go off the rails? That would upset the balance—an unpardonable sin."
—
Benoîte Groult, *Ainsi soit-elle*, 1975.

73

Article 17

Property belongs to both sexes, whether united or separated; for each of them this is an inviolable and sacred right; it is a legacy of nature and no one may be deprived of it unless there is a clear and legally determined public need, and then only on condition that fair and prior compensation is provided.

" 'A woman who is not afraid of men frightens them,' a young man once told me. And I have often heard adults declare: 'I cannot abide women taking the initiative.' If a woman offers herself too boldly, the man shies away. He insists on conquering. So the woman can take only when she makes herself prey: she must become a passive thing, a promise of submission. If she succeeds, she will believe that she has been a willing participant in this feat of conspiratorial magic and that she has reasserted her subjectivity. But she runs the risk of being frozen into a useless object by the male's disdain. This is why she is so deeply humiliated if she rejects his advances. The man may also become angry, believing that he has been taken in; however, he has simply failed in an endeavor, nothing more. The woman, on the other hand, has consented to become flesh through her excitement, anticipation, and expectation; she can win only by losing—and she remains lost. One must be ridiculously blind or exceptionally lucid to choose such a defeat."

—

Simone de Beauvoir, *The Second Sex*, 1949.

"A man who has a genuine fondness for women will let them freely use any weapon, as he finds so much pleasure in seeing women use them—even against himself."

—

Marcelle Auclair, *L'Amour, notes et maximes*, 1963.

"Women have served all these centuries as looking-glasses possessing the magic and delicious power of reflecting the figure of man at twice its natural size. Without that power probably the earth would still be swamp and jungle. The glories of all our wars would be unknown. We should still be scratching the outlines of deer on the remains of mutton bones and bartering flints for sheep skins or whatever simple ornament took our unsophisticated taste. Supermen and Fingers of Destiny would never have existed. The Czar and the Kaiser would never have worn crowns or lost them. Whatever may be their use in civilized societies, mirrors are essential to all violent and heroic action. That is why Napoleon and Mussolini both insist so emphatically upon the inferiority of women, for if they were not inferior, they would cease to enlarge. That serves to explain in part the necessity that women so often are to men. And it serves to explain how restless they are under her criticism; how impossible it is for her to say to them this book is bad, this picture is feeble, or whatever it may be, without giving far more pain and rousing far more anger than a man would do who gave the same criticism. For if she begins to tell the truth, the figure in the looking-glass shrinks; his fitness for life is diminished. How is he to go on giving judgement, civilizing natives, making laws, writing books, dressing up and speechifying at banquets, unless he can see himself at breakfast and at dinner at least twice the size he really is?"

—

Virginia Woolf, *A Room of One's Own*, 1929.

Postlude

Declaration of the Rights of Women and Female Citizens
by Olympe de Gouges

———

Woman, awake! The tocsin of reason is sounding across the universe; acknowledge your rights. Nature's powerful empire is no longer hemmed in by prejudice, fanaticism, superstition, and lies. The torch of truth has dispersed all the clouds of folly and usurpation. Enslaved man has multiplied his strength and has needed yours to break his chains. But once free, he has become unjust to his companion.

Oh women, women! When will you cease to be blind? What advantages has the Revolution brought you? Still greater contempt, still more overt disdain. In the centuries of corruption you ruled only over the weakness of men. Your empire has been destroyed; what remains to you now? A firm belief in the injustices of man. It is for you to reclaim your patrimony, founded on the wise decrees of nature; what have you to fear from such a magnificent undertaking? The remark by Christ at the wedding at Cana? Are you afraid that our French legislators, correctors of that morality long entangled in political practices that are now outdated, will say to you too: 'Woman, what is there in common between us?' 'Everything,' you must reply. Should they, in their weakness, persist in this non sequitur that contradicts their very principles, you must courageously counter these vain pretensions of superiority with the power of reason; you must unite under the banner of philosophy; deploy all your energy of character and you will soon see these arrogant men not groveling at your feet in servile adoration, but proud to share with you the treasures of the Supreme Being. Whatever barriers are placed before you, it is in your power to overcome them; all you need is the will.

Now let us turn to the appalling spectacle of what has been your role in society; and since national education is an issue of the moment, let us see whether our wise legislators will give reasonable thought to women's education.

Women have done more harm than good. Constraint and dissimulation have been their lot. What force has stolen from them, cunning has restored; they have resorted to all the resources of their charms and even the most upright of men have been unable to resist them. Poisoning, stabbing—everything was at their disposal and they commanded in crime as they did in virtue.

The French government depended for centuries on the nocturnal administrations of women; their indiscretion spared none of the cabinet's secrets: ambassadors, military commanders, ministers, presidents, pontiffs, cardinals—in short every office devised by the foolishness of men, both sacred and profane was fair game to the greed and ambition of this sex, once despicable yet respected and, since the Revolution, respectable yet despised. What volumes I could speak about this strange antithesis! But I have only this brief moment, though it is a moment that will seize the attention of every future generation. Under the old regime, everything was depraved, everyone was guilty; but can we not see an improvement in matters, in the very substance of these vices? A woman once needed only to be beautiful and charming; with these two advantages a hundred fortunes would fall at her feet. If she did not take advantage of them, her character was considered bizarre or she had a strange philosophy that gave her a disdain for wealth; in such cases, she was dismissed as 'difficult'; the most indecent woman could make herself respectable through wealth; the commerce in women was a kind of industry accepted in the upper classes but that henceforth will no longer enjoy credit. If it should continue to do so, the Revolution would be lost and even within this new order we would still be corrupt; however, can reason conceal the fact that every other way to fortune is closed to a woman bought by a man, like a slave on the coast of Africa? There is a great difference between them, as we know. The slave commands her master; but if the master gives her freedom without reward at an age when she has lost all her charms, what becomes of this unfortunate woman? She is an object of scorn; even the doors of charity are closed to her; she is poor and old, people say; why was she unable to make her fortune?

Other even more touching examples come to mind. A young, inexperienced girl seduced by a man she loves abandons her parents to follow him; after a few years, the ingrate leaves her and the older she has grown with him, the more inhuman his infidelity will be; if she has children, he will abandon her just the same. If he is rich, he will consider himself excused from sharing his fortune with his noble victims. If he is obliged to do his duty, he will disregard this obligation, counting on every support from the law. If he is married, all other commitments become void. What laws must yet be made to tear out such vice by its roots? A law that shares wealth between men and women and provides for it to be publicly administered.

It is easy to see that a woman born into a rich family has much to gain from an equal division. But what of a woman born into a poor family, who has merit and virtue, what becomes of her? Poverty and disgrace. Unless she excels in music or in painting, she cannot be admitted into any public function, even though she is perfectly capable. I wish here to give but a sketch of these things, which I will develop in detail in the new edition of my political writings, with supporting notes, that I intend to put before the public in a few days.

I return now to my discussion of morals. Marriage is the tomb of trust and love. A married woman can, with impunity, give bastard children to her husband, along with the fortune that does not rightly belong to them. An unmarried woman has very few rights: old, inhumane laws deny her children the right to their father's name and property and no new laws have been made in this respect. If seeking to give my sex credit for being honorable and just is considered paradoxical at this time, if it is seen as attempting the impossible, I shall leave to future men the glory of resolving this matter; meanwhile, we can prepare the way forward through national education, through the restoration of morals, and through conjugal agreements.

Illustrated by Anne-Lise Boutin

United Nations Declaration on the Elimination of Discrimination against Women

INTRODUCTION

—

Not only did Olympe de Gouges pay the highest price for her attacks on the patriarchy, she suffered, and continues to suffer, the ignominy of undeserved obscurity. These days, the "first wave" of feminism is generally understood to refer to the suffragettes and their contemporaries campaigning for equal electoral rights at the end of the nineteenth century and the beginning of the twentieth. De Gouges, who had publicly stood for the same principles, had been dead for over a century at that point.

Over the first half of the twentieth century, influenced by the arguments of those first-wave feminists, democratic nations afforded women ever better legal and electoral rights. This did not, though, mean that women's rights were making similar progress in either the domestic or wider cultural spheres. In that context, two global trends of the post-war period came to be expressed in the second of the texts we present here: the United Nations' Declaration on the Elimination of Discrimination against Women.

The first factor was the global growth of feminist thought and activism; the so-called "second wave" that addressed everyday issues like women's workplaces, sexuality, reproductive rights, domestic violence, and so on. At a grass-roots level, this cultural shift had—and continues to have—a huge impact on the lives and aspirations of ordinary women.

The second was the recognition, at a global political level, that addressing human rights in general would not be enough. In the aftermath of the global slaughter that was the Second World War, the UN was founded as an international body that would (amongst other aims) protect the human rights of individuals regardless of sex, race and religion. However, as the UN itself puts it, with considerable understatement, "the fact of women's humanity proved insufficient to guarantee them the enjoyment of their internationally agreed rights." In 1963, against a backdrop of second-wave feminist popular activism, the UN's Commission on the Status of Women was tasked with drafting a declaration that would have the moral and political force to improve women's lives worldwide, not only in the political sphere (for instance, the vote) but also the personal and domestic (it calls for an end to child marriages, and for equal educational opportunity).

The Declaration was issued in 1967: in 1979, it became the basis of the Convention on the Elimination of All Forms of Discrimination Against Women, now legally recognized in nearly every country in the world (everywhere except the Vatican, Iran, Somalia, Sudan, and Tonga). The descendant of one brave woman's polemic, written in a time of revolution, this now affects the lives of billions of women worldwide: an achievement and a legacy that should be celebrated, even as the struggle to improve women's lives, and achieve sex and gender equality, continues.

Preamble

(Resolution adopted by the General Assembly 2263 (XXII).
Declaration on the Elimination of Discrimination against Women)

—

Considering that the peoples of the United Nations have, in the Charter, reaffirmed their faith in fundamental human rights, in the dignity and worth of the human person and in the equal rights of men and women,

Considering that the Universal Declaration on Human Rights asserts the principle of non-discrimination and proclaims that all human beings are born free and equal in dignity and rights and that everyone is entitled to all the rights and freedoms set forth therein, without distinction of any kind, including any distinction as to sex,

Taking into account the resolutions, declarations, conventions, and recommendations of the United Nations and the specialized agencies designed to eliminate all forms of discrimination and to promote equal rights for men and women,

Concerned that, despite the Charter of the United Nations, the Universal Declaration of Human Rights, the International Covenants on Human Rights and other instruments of the United Nations and the specialized agencies and despite the progress made in the matter of equality of rights, there continues to exist considerable discrimination against women,

Considering that discrimination against women is incompatible with human dignity and with the welfare of the family and of society, prevents their participation, on equal terms with men, in the political, social, economic, and cultural life of their countries and is an obstacle to the full development of the potential of women in the service of their countries and of humanity,

Bearing in mind the great contribution made by women to social, political, economic, and cultural life and the part they play in the family and particularly in the rearing of children,

Convinced that the full and complete development of a country, the welfare of the world and the cause of peace require the maximum participation of women as well as men in all fields,

Considering that it is necessary to ensure the universal recognition in law and in fact of the principle of equality of men and women,

Solemnly proclaims this Declaration.

Article 1

Discrimination against women, denying or limiting as it does their equality of rights with men, is fundamentally unjust and constitutes an offence against human dignity.

Illustrated by Amélie Falière

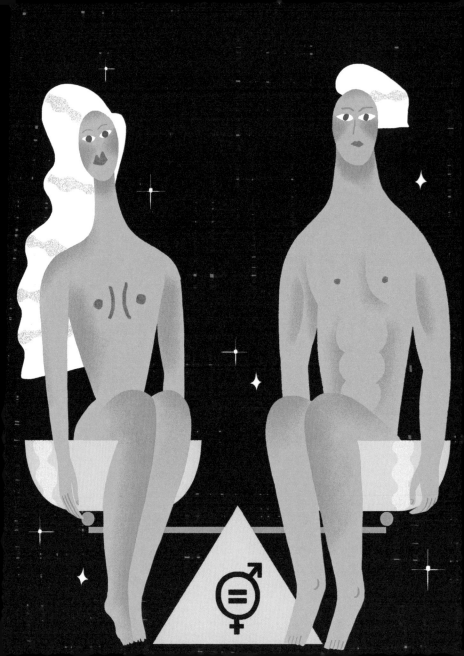

"It is a violation of human rights when babies are denied food, or drowned, or suffocated, or their spines broken, simply because they are born girls. It is a violation of human rights when women and girls are sold into the slavery of prostitution for human greed. It is a violation of human rights when women are doused with gasoline, set on fire, and burned to death because their marriage dowries are deemed too small. It is a violation of human rights when individual women are raped in their own communities and when thousands of women are subjected to rape as a tactic or prize of war. It is a violation of human rights when a leading cause of death worldwide among women ages 14 to 44 is the violence they are subjected to in their own homes by their own relatives. It is a violation of human rights when young girls are brutalized by genital mutilation. It is a violation of human rights when women are denied the right to plan their own families, and that includes being forced to have abortions or being sterilized against their will. If there is one message that echoes forth from this conference, let it be that human rights are women's rights and women's rights are human rights once and for all."

—

Hillary Clinton, speech given at the UN 4th World Conference on Women, Beijing, September 5, 1995.

"For as long as this equality is not universally recognized and concretely realized, it is very difficult for a woman to act as an equal to a man."
—
Simone de Beauvoir, *The Second Sex*, 1949.

"Sexism is even deeper and more endemic than racism."
—
Benoîte Groult, *Ainsi soit-elle*, 1975.

"For a man to think he can fulfill his destiny without woman is a blunder, a misunderstanding, a miscalculation, a false move; it is reckless folly and doomed to failure. Of course, woman is not everything, but everything depends on her… Look around you. Look at history. Stop and consider the whole world and tell me—what are men without women? What wishes, what prayers do they have that are not in praise of woman? Whether rich as Croesus or poor as Job, slaves or tyrants, if woman were to turn her back on us, no horizon would be vast enough to satisfy our gaze."
—
Yasmina Khadra, *What the Day Owes the Night*, 2008.

Article 2

All appropriate measures shall be taken
to abolish existing laws, customs,
regulations, and practices which are
discriminatory against women,
and to establish adequate legal protection
for equal rights of men and women,
in particular:
a) The principle of equality
of rights shall be embodied
in the constitution or otherwise
guaranteed by law;
b) The international instruments
of the United Nations and the
specialized agencies relating to
the elimination of discrimination
against women shall be ratified or
acceded to and fully implemented
as soon as practicable.

Illustrated by Sébastien Mourrain

"Men and citizens, in our pride, more than once we have said: the eighteenth century proclaimed the rights of men; the nineteenth will proclaim the rights of women. But, citizens, we must admit we have been far from hasty; many considerations, of a serious nature, I concede, and that required careful reflection, have held us back. And as I speak now, at the point of progress we have reached, there are among the finest Republicans and the truest, purest Democrats many excellent minds that still hesitate to accept the equality of the human soul in man and woman and therefore that their civil rights should be similar if not indeed identical."

—

Victor Hugo, "At the grave of Louise Julien, speech given at Saint-Jean Cemetery," Jersey, July 26, 1853.

"What! Do women not have the same passions, the same needs as men? Are they not subject to the same physical laws? And yet supposedly they do not have the intelligence needed to curb and govern their instincts? Give women duties as difficult as those given to men, subject them to moral and social laws that are just as severe, and will they not demonstrate just as full and free a will and a reasoning mind just as lucid and apt for education? God and men are to blame here. They have committed a crime because they have placed on earth and tolerated a race whose true and complete existence is impossible. If woman is inferior to man, let us then sever all links, no longer impose on her faithfulness in love or legitimate motherhood; let us even abolish for her those laws regarding safety of life and security of property; let us make war on her without further ado. Laws whose purpose and spirit she is supposedly incapable of grasping as fully as those who create them are absurd laws; if this were the case there would be no reason not to subject domestic animals to human legislation too."

—

George Sand, "Sixth Letter to Marcie," *Le Monde*, March 27, 1837.

"The majority of those who take up the cause of women against men's arrogant preconception that they are superior, would turn the whole thing round, transferring this superiority to women. For myself, preferring to shun all extremes, I am happy to see women as equal to men—Nature, in this respect, being opposed to both superiority and inferiority."

—

Marie de Gournay, *Égalité des hommes et des femmes*, 1622.

"The admission of women to full equality would be the most convincing mark of civilization; it would double the intellectual strength of the human race and its chances of achieving happiness."

—

Stendhal, *Rome, Naples and Florence*, June 19, 1817.

Article 3

All appropriate
measures shall be taken
to educate public opinion
and to direct national
aspirations toward
the eradication of prejudice
and the abolition
of customary and all
other practices which are
based on the idea of the
inferiority of women.

Illustrated by Céline Gobinet

"For as long as women are unable to walk around or work and be treated with respect, without having to constantly think, even secretly, about defending their personal, mental, or physical space, such behavior—whistling, making inappropriate remarks—will need to be condemned."
—
Natacha Henry, *Les Mecs lourds ou le Paternalisme lubrique*, 2003.

"To be female in this place is to be an open wound that cannot heal. Even if scars form, the festering is ever below."
—
Toni Morrison, *A Mercy*, 2009.

"A feminist anthropologist [...] told them about her research on rape in the animal kingdom. Nearly every species had some form of rape, she said, except for the bonobos, a group of primates similar to chimpanzees. Somewhere along the line, the female bonobos decided that they would no longer tolerate sexual violence. So when a male attacked one of them, she emitted a sound to draw attention to herself. The other female bonobos would drop what they were doing, rush toward the sound, and together they would tear the offending male limb from limb. [...] Why couldn't women be more like that?"
—
J. Courtney Sullivan, *Commencement*, 2013.

"Since the end of the eighteenth century, when, as we have seen, imprisonment began to emerge as the dominant form of punishment, convicted women have been represented as essentially different from their male counterparts. It is true that men who commit the kinds of transgressions that are regarded as punishable by the state are labeled as social deviants. Nevertheless, masculine criminality has always been deemed more 'normal' than feminine criminality. There has always been a tendency to regard those women who have been publicly punished by the state for their misbehaviors as significantly more aberrant and far more threatening to society than their numerous male counterparts.

In seeking to understand this gendered difference in the perception of prisoners, it should be kept in mind that as the prison emerged and evolved as the major form of public punishment, women continued to be routinely subjected to forms of punishment that have not been acknowledged as such. For example, women have been incarcerated in psychiatric institutions in greater proportions than in prisons."

—

Angela Davis, *Is Prison Obsolete?*, 2014.

Article 4

All appropriate measures shall be taken to ensure women are on equal terms with men, without any discrimination:
a) The right to vote in all elections and be eligible for election to all publicly elected bodies;
b) The right to vote in all public referenda;
c) The right to hold public office and to exercise all public functions.

Such rights shall be guaranteed by legislation.

Illustrated by Éric Gosselet

"It is painful to say it but in civilization today, there is a slave. The law uses euphemisms: What I call a slave, it calls a minor; according to the law, this minor—in reality a slave—is woman. Man has loaded the scales of the law unevenly, yet its balance is important to human consciousness; man has placed all the rights on his side and all the duties on woman's side, thus creating profound disruption. Creating female servitude. Under our laws, as they stand at present, woman cannot enjoy ownership; she cannot go to court; she cannot vote; she does not count; she does not exist. There are male citizens; there are no female citizens. This is a violent state and it must cease."
—
Victor Hugo, letter to Léon Richer, June 8, 1872.

"Women will make children when they have the right to vote, by which I mean when they are able, like men, to decide on peace and war."
—
Marguerite Durand, *Lecture notes on votes for women*, undated [1927].

"The enemy is not men. The enemy is the concept of patriarchy. The concept of patriarchy as the way to run the world or do things."
—
Toni Morrisson, *Conversations*, 2008.

"This ignoramus who can neither read nor write, who is incapable of telling his right from his left and so is ordered to mark his army boots so that he can tell them apart, who marches blindly to the tune of 'Left! Right! … Left! Right!'—this ignoramus is entitled to vote. This oaf who whips and beats his horses, mindlessly, pitilessly, without even the slightest concern for his own interests; who indiscriminately hands out injustice and suffering—this oaf is entitled to vote. This drunkard who drinks from dawn to dusk and from evening to morning, this drunken, hiccupping, slobbering semblance of a man who has left his reason at the bottom of the first glass, so intoxicated that he ricochets from one wall to another, wallowing in his own excrement—this drunkard is entitled to vote. Voters too are the layabout whose wife must feed him, the lout who lives off his daughter, the doddery old fool who has worn himself out with debauchery, the half mad fool, and the madman who claims to be cured. The idiot master of the world—he too is a voter! Yet woman, deemed to be inferior to all these, has no role to play but taxpayer; but one single duty—to pay; but one single right—to be silent."
–

Séverine, quoted by Léon Aumeran in the newspaper *Le Progrés de Bel-Abbès*, May 25, 1910.

Article 5

Women shall have
the same rights
as men to acquire,
change or retain
their nationality.
Marriage to an alien
shall not automatically
affect the nationality
of the wife either by
rendering her stateless
or by forcing upon her the
nationality of her husband.

Illustrated by Nathalie Ragondet

"This concept of marriage is a disgrace! The wife as property of the husband! She does not even have the right to call herself by her real name! She has to bear the husband's mark of ownership branded on her forehead! Like an animal!"

—

Albert Cohen, *Belle du Seigneur*, 1968.

"I realized that the wife is not the husband's bondslave, but his companion and his helpmate, and an equal partner in all his joys and sorrows—as free as the husband to choose her own path."

—

Mahatma Gandhi, *All Men Are Brothers*, 1942–1956.

"Man is the only animal who injures his mate."

—

Ludovico Ariosto, *Orlando Furioso*, 1516.

"In the first place, the opinion in favor of the present system, which entirely subordinates the weaker sex to the stronger, rests upon theory only; for there never has been trial made of any other: so that experience, in the sense in which it is vulgarly opposed to theory, cannot be pretended to have announced any verdict. And in the second place, the adoption of this system of inequality never was the result of deliberation, or forethought, or any social ideas or any notion whatever of what conduced to the benefit of humanity or the good order of society. It arose simply from the fact that from the very earliest twilight of human society, every woman (owing to the value attached to her by men, combined with her inferiority in muscular strength) was found in a state of bondage to some man. Laws and systems of polity always begin by recognizing the relations they already find existing between individuals. They convert what was a mere physical fact into a legal right, give it the sanction of society and principally aim at the substitution of public and organized means of asserting and protecting these rights, instead of the irregular and lawless conflict of physical strength. Those who had already been compelled to obedience became in this manner legally bound to it."
–
John Stuart Mill, *The Subjection of Women*, 1869.

Article 6

1. Without prejudice to the safeguarding of the unity
and the harmony of the family, which remains the basic unit
of any society, all appropriate measures, particularly legislative
measures, shall be taken to ensure to women,
married or unmarried, equal rights with men in the field
of civil law, and in particular:
a) The right to acquire, administer, enjoy, dispose of and inherit
property, including property acquired during marriage;
b) The right to equality in legal capacity and the exercise thereof;
c) The same rights as men with regard to the law
on the movement of persons.

2. All appropriate measures shall be taken to ensure
the principle of equality of status of the husband and wife,
and in particular:
a) Women shall have the same right as men to free choice
of a spouse and to enter into marriage only with their free
and full consent;
b) Women shall have equal rights with men during marriage
and at its dissolution. In all cases the interest of the children
shall be paramount;
c) Parents shall have equal rights and duties in matters
relating to their children. In all cases the interest of
the children shall be paramount.

3. Child marriage and the betrothal of young girls
before puberty shall be prohibited, and effective action,
including legislation, shall be taken to specify a minimum age
for marriage and to make the registration of marriages
in an official registry compulsory.

Illustrated by Paul Echegoyen

"Some might claim that servitude has been abolished in civilized Europe. It is true that slave markets are no longer held in public places; nevertheless, among even the most advanced countries, there is not one in which several classes of individuals do not still suffer oppression under the law. Peasants in Russia, Jews in Rome, sailors in England—and women everywhere; yes, everywhere that the cessation of mutual consent, necessary to the formation of marriage, is insufficient to end it, woman is in servitude. Only divorce obtained at the express will of one of the parties can free her, can place her on a level with man, at least in terms of civil rights."
—
Flora Tristan, *Pérégrinations d'une paria*, 1833–1834.

"To sum up the boldness of my thinking, it is to demand divorce in marriage. I have thought long and hard and, for me, the only remedy to the mortal injustices, to the endless miseries, to the often incurable passions that disrupt the union of the sexes is the freedom to break conjugal ties and form them again. I do not believe that divorce should be resorted to lightly or with motives any less serious than those required for obtaining legal separation as now apply. Although, for my part, I should prefer to spend the rest of my life in a dungeon rather than marry again, I know of instances of such durable, such imperative affection that no ancient civil or religious law could act as a lasting restraint. And we must always remember that affection becomes stronger and worthier as the human intellect is refined and purified."
—
George Sand, letter to Abbé de Lamennais, Nohant, February 28, 1837.

"The modern family unit is founded on the domestic slavery of the wife, whether visible or concealed, and modern society is a mass composed of such family units, as any mass is composed of molecules. In the great majority of cases today, or at least in the property-owning classes, the husband is obliged to earn a living and provide for his family, and that in itself gives him a position of supremacy without the need for special legal titles and privileges. Within the family he is the bourgeois, and the wife represents the proletariat. But in the industrial world, the specific character of the economic oppression burdening the proletariat is visible in all its sharpness only when all special legal privileges of the capitalist class have been abolished and complete legal equality of both classes established. The democratic republic does not do away with the opposition of the two classes; on the contrary, it provides the field on which the fight can be fought out. And in the same way, the peculiar nature of the supremacy of the husband over the wife in the modern family, as well as the necessity for real social equality between them and the means to achieve it, will be seen in the clear light of day only when both legally possess completely equal rights. Then it will be plain that the first condition for the liberation of the wife is to bring the whole female sex back into public industry, and that this in turn demands that the family unit cease to be the fundamental economic unit of society."

—

Friedrich Engels, after notes by Karl Marx, *The Origin of the Family, Private Property and the State*, 1884.

All provisions of penal codes which constitute discrimination against women shall be repealed.

Illustrated by Daphné Hong

"What is it that women want? It really is quite simple. They want everything that all oppressed, subjugated people have wanted since society began: their fair share of rights and freedoms. […] Peoples who have found no guarantees in their leaders' promises have always wanted their rights; and this is what women want.

One might argue that they have been tardy in asserting this; and that if their social inferiority has lasted so long, why should it not continue for longer still? No progress is immediate, as the word itself implies: people have been fighting, battling, arguing to gain their freedom for more than six thousand years, and yet much remains to be done. Only when the day came that tradition was toppled, when questions were asked, and women's true value was recognized, only then did the people begin to doubt the legitimacy of this absolute royal power. They looked mistrustfully at these so-called lieutenants of God; they ceased to believe that they had been put on earth simply to obey and serve. And what happened once with these peoples is now happening with women.

Once tradition is challenged, woman throws off her yoke. Her faith had made her accept being punished for an offense that she could barely remember committing; she believed herself to be culpable, but not incapable; she resigned herself to subjection, to humiliation so that one day she would bathe in the glory of God.

But now, she refuses to believe that biting an apple without permission, in a search for knowledge—that most noble of desires—was sufficient for her and all those women who followed her to merit mistreatment in the centuries to come.

Such is the progress of ideas."
—
Maria Deraismes (1828–1894), "Ce que veulent les femmes," *Le Droit des femmes*, no. 1, April 10 1869.

"We have to free half of the human race, the women, so that they can help to free the other half."
—
Emmeline Pankhurst, quoted in the UN Human Development Report (UNDP), 2013.

"Two centuries after the Declaration of Human Rights, we are still having to fight for it to apply to the whole of the human race."
—
Benoîte Groult, *Ainsi soit-elle*, 1975.

"Today, the time has come for us to pull together, to restore to feminism its true foundation and its universalist vocation as women of the left fighting for the rights of all women, wherever they may be and whatever their origin or their color, always mindful that there must be laws in place to safeguard freedom of conscience and prevent communitarian laws and rules from allowing patriarchy to reassert itself."
—
Algerian and Iranian Secular Feminists Collective, *Open letter to our female feminist friends*, 2016.

Article 8

Appropriate measures,
including legislation,
shall be taken
to combat all forms
of traffic in women
and exploitation
of prostitution
of women.

Illustrated by Carlos Felipe León

"In the interests of safeguarding the bourgeois family, the breeding ground of the heirs to capital, trade in the female body is encouraged, although, from the viewpoint of 'official morals,' it is severely and mercilessly condemned; and to maintain in its own eyes its reputation of 'high moral purity,' bourgeois society is quick to accuse prostitutes of outraging its apparent virtue and takes every opportunity to poison the already wretched existence of these unfortunate 'priestesses of vice.'"

—
Alexandra Kollontaï, "The Problems of Prostitution," *La Bataille socialiste*, 1909.

"Are there not street markets where in pavement displays, the pretty daughters of the people are sold, while the daughters of the rich are sold for their dowry? The first are taken by whoever wants them; the second are given to whoever their family may wish. The prostitution is the same."

—
Louise Michel, *Mémoires de Louise Michel écrits par elle-même*, 1886.

"Even from our egotistic viewpoint, we recognize that it is difficult to balance the happiness of man against the suffering of woman."

—
Victor Hugo, Letter to Léon Richer, June 8, 1872.

"For them, adultery is worse than murder. But not all types of adultery: adultery committed by a man is not punished at all. Whereas adultery by a woman is considered to be the end of the world."

—
Djemila Benhabib, *Les Soldats d'Allah à l'assaut de l'Occident*, 2011.

"Men have made a magnificent distinction, to which they hold fast, between their own women—duty, motherhood, halo-wearing, headache— and other women—pleasure, prostitution, provocation, damnation…"

—
Françoise Giroud, *Si je mens*, 1972.

Article 9

All appropriate measures shall be taken to ensure
to girls and women, married or unmarried, equal rights
with men in education at all levels, and in particular:
a) Equal conditions of access to, and study in,
educational institutions of all types, including universities
and vocational, technical, and professional schools;
b) The same choice of curricula, the same examinations,
teaching staff with qualifications of the same standard,
and school premises and equipment of the same quality,
whether the institutions are co-educational or not;
c) Equal opportunities to benefit from scholarships
and other study grants;
d) Equal opportunities for access to programs
of continuing education, including adult
literacy programs;
e) Access to educational information to help
in ensuring the health and well-being of families.

Illustrated by Sandrine Han Jin Kuang

"Education must be the same for women as for men. […] Indeed, since all education is designed to expose truth, to develop the proof of this truth, it is hard to see why a difference of gender should require a difference in the choice of these truths, or in the manner of proving them."
—
Nicolas de Condorcet, *Cinq Mémoires sur l'instruction publique*, 1791.

"It's clear that a complete woman, who has both sexuality and intelligence, is difficult to take."
—
Erica Jong, *In conversation with Sophie Lannes*, July–August 1978.

"Equal rights and mixed schools have not been enough to put an end to the difference in the way that girls and boys are seen, the gender construct of academic paths, and sexist violence at school."
—
Vincent Peillon and Najat Vallaud-Belkacem, "Pour plus d'égalité entre filles et garçons à l'école," *Le Monde*, September 25, 2012.

"We demand full freedom and a complete education for women."
—
Jeanne Loiseau, aka Daniel-Lesueur, *L'Évolution féminine, ses résultats économiques*, 1905.

"In this profound silence, women are not alone. It envelops a lost continent of lives swallowed up by the oblivion into which the mass of humanity vanishes. But it weighs far more heavily on women, because of the inequality of the sexes, what Françoise Héritier calls the 'differential valency' that structures society's past. This is at the root of the second ineqality: the poor traceability of women, which makes it so difficult—though to a varying extent depending on the period—to situate them across time. Because they appear less in the public sphere, a major subject of observation and narrative, they are mentioned little and even less so if the narrator is a man accustomed to their habitual absence, to the use of a universal masculine, to globalizing stereotypes or the supposed unicity of the female gender. The lack of concrete, circumstantial information is in contrast with the abundance of discourse and the profusion of images. Women are imagined far more than described or recounted, and to tell their story means first and inevitably to come up against this stumbling block of representations that masks them and needs to be analyzed, without knowing how they saw these themselves or how they experienced them […]."
—
Michelle Perrot, *Les Femmes ou les Silences de l'histoire*, 1998.

Article 10

1. All appropriate measures shall be taken to ensure to women, married or unmarried, equal rights with men in the field of economic and social life, and in particular:
a) The right, without discrimination on grounds of marital status or any other grounds, to receive vocational training, to work, to free choice of profession and employment, and to professional and vocational advancement;
b) The right to equal remuneration with men and to equality of treatment in respect of work of equal value;
c) The right to leave with pay, retirement privileges and provision for security in respect of unemployment, sickness, old age or other incapacity to work;
d) The right to receive family allowances on equal terms with men.

2. In order to prevent discrimination against women on account of marriage or maternity and to ensure their effective right to work, measures shall be taken to prevent their dismissal in the event of marriage or maternity and to provide paid maternity leave, with the guarantee of returning to former employment, and to provide the necessary social services, including child-care facilities.

3. Measures taken to protect women in certain types of work, for reasons inherent in their physical nature, shall not be regarded as discriminatory.

Illustrated by Stéphane Kardos

"Whatever women do they must do twice as well as men to be thought half as good. Luckily this is not difficult."
—
Charlotte Whitton, in *Canada Month*, June 1963.

"Women can do anything a man can do, except pee against a wall standing up."
—
Colette (1873–1954).

"It is through work that woman has been able, to a large extent, to close the gap separating her from the male; work alone can guarantee her concrete freedom."
—
Simone de Beauvoir, *The Second Sex*, 1949.

"Although we weren't able to shatter that highest, hardest glass ceiling this time, thanks to you, it's got about 18 million cracks in it, and the light is shining through like never before, filling us all with the hope and the sure knowledge that the path will be a little easier next time."
—
Hillary Clinton, speech given at the National Building Museum, Washington, June 7, 2008.

"Woman will truly be the equal of man on the day an important post is awarded to an incompetent woman."
—
Françoise Giroud (1916–2003).

Article 11

1. The principle of equality of rights
of men and women demands
implementation in all States
in accordance with the principles
of the Charter of the United Nations
and of the Universal Declaration
of Human Rights.

2. Governments, non-governmental
organizations and individuals
are urged, therefore, to do all
in their power to promote
the implementation of
the principles contained
in this Declaration.

Illustrated by Christophe Lautrette

\

Artist Biographies

\

Declaration of the Rights of Women and Female Citizens by Olympe de Gouges

Prelude

Gérald Guerlais was born in Nantes in 1974 and graduated from the French National School of Applied Arts. He illustrates for the press (Bayard, Prisma, Milan) and children's literature, including the *Les Petits Monstres* series—Père Castor/Flammarion, Fleurus, Gautier-Languereau, Deux Coqs d'or, and Penguin Books. He also works in animated set design for French and American studios (Futurikon, Gaumont Animation, Xilam, Sony).

With a passion for cultural exchange, Gérald created the international charity art project Sketchtravel. He is a monthly columnist for the art magazine *L'Œil*. In the United States he is represented by the KidShannon agency.

www.geraldguerlais.com

Article 1

Camille André was born in 1990 in South Korea. With a high school diploma in literature, she continued her studies in movie animation at ESAAT in Roubaix, then at the Gobelins School of Visual Arts in Paris.

Camille began her career with American studios (Sony Pictures Animation, Blue Sky Studios) and for a time worked for Disney France. Now in Paris, she collaborates with the Onyx Film studio as a character designer and alongside this is developing a comic book project.

cephalon-art.blogspot.fr
facebook.com/camille.andre.art

Article 2

Lionel Richerand was born prematurely in La Tronche in the Isère region of France in the early 1970s. His means of expression is drawing. After training at the Penninghen School of Graphic Arts and at the School of Decorative Arts in Paris, in 2001 he produced a 26-minute puppet movie, *La Peur du loup*; in 2003 he co-produced the series *Les Grabonautes* as well as contributing to the feature-length movie *Renaissance* by Christian Volckman. He also works as an illustrator for publishers Bayard and Milan and is producing an illustrated book—*L'Étrange Réveillon*, based on a text by Bertrand Santini—for Grasset Jeunesse.

His comic books include *Petit Conte léguminesque* published by Akileos, *Les Nouveaux Pirates* with La Joie de Lire, and *Dans la forêt* with Éditions Soleil ("Métamorphose" collection). Lionel is currently working on various new comic book projects.

facebook.com/LionelRicherand

Article 3

Luc Desmarchelier was born in Lyon in 1965. After spending a few years in advertising in Lyon and Martinique, he began working in animation as a layout artist in 1990, first in Paris, then in London, and finally in Los Angeles, where he became an artistic director with Dreamworks Animation and Sony Pictures Animation.

He has worked on animated feature-length movies including *The Prince of Egypt*, *The Road to Eldorado*, *Shrek*, *Spirit*, *Corpse Bride*, *Open Season*, and *Hotel Transylvania*, as well as on movies such as *The Cat in the Hat*, *Charlie and the Chocolate Factory*, and *Tomorrowland*.

Luc is currently working freelance and also teaches illustration and visual development at the Laguna College of Art and Design in California. His professional and personal work is available on blogs and his interest in silver-based photography and art photography can be found on his Flickr page.

ldesmarchelier.com
ushuaiasblog.blogspot.com
harmattansblog.blogspot.com
flickr.com/photos/harmattangallery

Article 4

A painter and cartoonist living in Brittany, **Hugues Mahoas** quickly made a name for himself in the world of animation. For a number of years he has contributed to the successful animated series *Les Zinzins de l'Espace* and *La Famille Pirate*. But it is his own 52-episode series *La Vache, le Chat et l'Océan* that has made him famous. Hugues also writes for children.

mahoas.blogspot.fr

Article 5

Yrgane Ramon works for European publishers and the European press, and her work includes comic books and advertising. She also teaches at the Émile-Cohl Art School in Lyon and is a tattoo artist.

yrgane.com

Article 6

Louis Thomas is a director and illustrator. He graduated from the Gobelins School of Visual Arts in Paris, and from CalArts in Los Angeles at the end of 2012. After an exchange year and contracts with animation studios in California, he decided to move back to France to give himself more freedom in his work.

Since 2013, he has been living and working—with the help of his cat Pipo—in a studio between the Panthéon and the Luxembourg Gardens in Paris. For his different productions, he likes to collaborate with animators trained at the Gobelins School and composer and sound designer friends.

Recent clients include Pixar, Universal, Cartoon Network, Laika, Sony Pictures, Thames and Hudson, Havas, Intersport, L'École des loisirs, Bayard, Penguin, and Random House.

louist.blogspot.fr

Article 7

Maël Gourmelen is an animator, designer, and illustrator. After studying graphic art and illustration at the Brassart School in Tours, he graduated from the Gobelins School of Visual Arts in Paris in 2008. He alternates between Paris (with Universal) and Los Angeles, where he lived and worked for two years with Disney Studios and DreamWorks Animation, bringing hand-drawn characters to life.

At the end of 2013, he moved back to Paris with his wife to develop his work on a freelance basis and extend his client base, which now includes the Laika, Aardman, and Paramount Animation studios. Alongside this, he is gradually moving into illustration and production.

Maël is passionate about nature and animals.

grudoaaameriques.blogspot.fr

Article 8

Maly Siri was born in France in 1985, but has lived in Canada for several years. She specializes in pin-up art, bringing a softer and more feminist vision to the style. Far from objectifying women, she produces female characters who are full of confidence in themselves and their desirability. Her latest book, *Maly Siri's Pin-up Art*, published by Éditions Soleil, is a 2-books-in-1 collection (*Good Girls vs Bad Girls*) combining fresh, light-hearted illustrations with captivating, dark images—all set in a glamorous world inspired by the 1930s to 1960s.

Article 9

Born on October 8, 1985, in Châtenay-Malabry in the Paris region, **Maïlys Vallade** was quick to show an interest in graphic arts and stop motion.

She began her training at a high school for applied arts, followed by the School of Graphic Art and Animation, and then the Gobelins School, where she was part of a team that produced two short animated films—*Garuda* and *The Lighthouse Keeper*—both of which won prizes, including the 2010 Cristal d'Annecy student film award; she also directed *L'Ermite* as a solo production.

Maïlys works mainly in animated film, primarily as a storyboarder on feature-length movies such as *The Little Prince, Long Way North, Un homme est mort,* and *The Swallows of Kabul.* She has also worked as an animator on *Ernest & Celestine, Long Way North, The Twilight Hour,* and *Silex and the City,* and in visual development and set design on *The Swallows of Kabul, Adama: Le Monde des Souffles,* and *Lascars, the film.* She is developing short movie drawn animation and stop-motion projects.

Maïlys also works as a graffiti and stop-motion artist employing a wide range of tools and materials and is involved in various group illustration projects, often for charity.

mailysvallade.blogspot.fr

133

Article 10

Wassim Boutaleb J. was born in Morocco in 1985 and grew up in Paris. Graduating in animated film direction from the Gobelins School of Visual Arts in June 2008, he has now made this his profession. At the same time, a desire to tell his own stories has led him toward illustration and comic books. He works for *Tchô Mag* and *Astrapi* and is illustrating a novel for *J'aime Lire*. *La Team* is his first comic book.

Article 11

Marc Lizano was born in Vannes, in Brittany, in 1970 and takes equal pleasure in working for the press, in children's publishing, and on comic books.

Following the successful release of *The Island of Thirty Coffins*, *The Hidden Child* (translated into 6 languages, 23 prizes) and a complete reissue of *La Petite Famille* in 2015, he has worked on *Marcelin Comète* (with Élodie Shanta), an adaptation of *The Horse of Pride* by Pierre-Jakez Hélias (with Bertrand Galic), *Die Neue Geschichten von Vater & Sohn*, based on the book Vater & Sohn by E.O. Plauen (with Ulf K.), *La Pension Moreau* (alongside Benoît Broyart), and *Arsène Lupin* (with Joël Legars).

Marc sometimes draws kangaroos in the zoo at the Jardin des Plantes—until 5pm.

marc-lizano.weebly.com

Carole Trébor is a French writer for children and young people. She has also worked as a historian and documentary movie maker. Following the success of her series *Nina Volkovitch* (four volumes published by Gulfstream), she was part of the 2015 fall Nathan-Syros literary event and is now writing *Svetlana*, which will be published by Rageot.

minisites-charte.fr/sites/carole-trebor
fr.wikipedia.org/wiki/Carole_Trébor

Article 12

Sébastien Pelon lives and works in Paris. He is a graphic artist and illustrator who graduated from the Duperré School of Applied Arts in graphic design, fashion, and the environment. After a few years with the Père Castor Flammarion studio, he is now freelance and works with Flammarion, Rue de Sèvres, Nathan, Magnard, Milan, Auzou, Rageot, Gallimard, and others.

Sébastien has illustrated numerous children's books, classic tales, and series, including *Matriochka*, *La Befana*, *La Mamani*, *Robin des bois*, *Sinbad le Marin*, *Nitou l'Indien*, and *Brune du Lac*.

sebastienpelon.com

Article 13

Jazzi studied at the Strasbourg School of Decorative Arts and specialized in illustration at the Claude Lapointe studio. He worked for two years as a set designer for edutainment CD-Roms (for Vivendi Universal), then became an illustrator for the press and children's publications.

He publishes regularly with various publishers including Hachette, Hatier, Nathan, Fleurus Presse, and Bayard. Since 2009, he has been sharing his passion for drawing by teaching illustration at the CESAN Art School in Paris.

jazzillus.canalblog.com
jazzi.ultra-book.com

—

Article 14

Aurélien Prédal was born in 1984 in Suresnes and studied at the Gobelins School of Visual Arts in Paris. Aurélien co-produced *Burning Safari*, a 3D short student movie shown at the Annecy Festival in 2006. He works regularly on a freelance basis for Onyx Film, DreamWorks, Laika, Nickelodeon, Sony Animation, and the Aardman studios.

aurelien-predal.blogspot.fr

Article 15

Aude Massot was born in 1983 in Les Lilas, Paris. She graduated in cartoon art from the St-Luc School in Brussels and began her career as an animation storyboarder. Her first book, *Chronique d'une chair grillée*, produced in collaboration with Fabien Bertrand, was published by Les Enfants Rouges in 2009. This was followed by two further books.`

In 2011, she spent a year in Montreal, where she met scriptwriters Édouard Bourré-Guilbert and Pauline Bardin, and became the artist for *Québec Land*. This went digital in May 2013, enjoying great success on the web, before going into print with publishers Éditions Sarbacane.

www.odemasso.com

Article 16

Kness studied some fascinating but rather impractical subjects before deciding that her vocation was to draw ponies. So she became an illustrator—and more.

Kness is also a cook, is raising a little corgi and a beautiful baby, is creating an organic vegetable garden, and... is something of a magician, managing to combine all this with the more serious role of project manager (which means putting on glasses and frowning a bit).

kness.net

Article 17

Yasmine Gateau studied at the HEAR Art School of the Rhine in Strasbourg, where she specialized in stage design. She went on to work with various theater and dance companies.

In 2007, she began producing illustrations for children's books. She now works for the press and the publishing and communications industries. Her illustrations appear regularly in the French and international press (*Le Monde*, *XXI*, *Variety*, etc).

yasminegateau.com

Postlude

Anne-Lise Boutin has lived and worked in Paris since 1995. She graduated from the Duperré School of Applied Arts in art and textile printing and from the French National School of Decorative Arts in Paris, where she studied "the image and the news." She now works extensively for the press and also produces book covers. Her oil pastel and cut paper illustrations take their inspiration from Mexican *calaveras* and other strange and wonderful things.

anneliseboutin.blogspot.fr

United Nations Declaration on the Elimination of Discrimination against Women

Article 1

After studying visual communication at the École Estienne in Paris, **Amélie Falière** decided to follow her dream and become an illustrator. Taking inspiration from the illustrators of the 1950s and UPA (an American animation style in vogue in the 1960s), she aims for a graphic style that is simple, uncluttered, and above all colorful.

ameliefaliere.ultra-book.com

Article 2

Sébastien Mourrain was born in Aubervilliers in 1976. He studied at the Émile-Cohl School of Applied Arts in Lyon, graduating in 2000. Having decided to become an illustrator, he now works for a number of publishers (including Actes Sud Junior, Les Fourmis rouges, and Seuil Jeunesse) as well as for the press. He exhibits his work via Imagier Vagabond and lives in Lyon, where he is part of the Bocal studio.

sebastienmourrain.tumblr.com

Article 3

As a child, **Céline Gobinet** avoided boredom by spending her time drawing and making up stories. After a school career in which drawing always played an important part, she became a student at the Gobelins Film Animation School in 1995. There she decided to specialize in storyboarding, which has allowed her to continue to tell and draw stories for animated series and feature films.

cgobinet.blogspot.fr

Article 4

Éric Gosselet aka Mister EGG
directs animated movies
(Gaumont-Marathon). Between
productions he illustrates for
the press (Milan) and publishers
(Akileos-Bang Ediciones).

mister-egg.blogspot.fr

—

Article 5

Nathalie Ragondet is a young
illustrator who graduated from
the Émile-Cohl School of Applied
Arts in Lyon. She enjoys mixing
watercolor and gouache. She lives
in the Drôme region of France.

www.tumblr.com/tagged/nathalie-
ragondet

Article 6

After completing a high school
diploma in science and studying
at Tarbes Drawing Academy, **Paul
Echegoyen** moved to Paris in
2003 to further pursue his studies
at the Penninghen School of
Graphic Art.

After graduating in 2008 and
spending a few years as a
freelance graphic artist and
storyboarder, he illustrated his
first children's book for Éditions
du Seuil Jeunesse in October 2011.
Since then he has worked on other
children's books and comic books
(for the Éditions Soleil
"Noctambule" collection), as well
as for the press (notably for the
Dada magazine's *Ieno 19*—a tribute
to Hayao Miyazaki).

He regularly exhibits his work, in
particular at the Daniel Maghen
(Paris), Arludik (Paris), and Nucleus
(Los Angeles) galleries.

He has a special interest in
ecology, childhood nostalgia,
and the dream world of the
imagination. Paul uses a variety of
techniques in his book illustration,
ranging from watercolor to
gouache, but also including
graphite and colored pencil.

paulechegoyen.tumblr.com

Article 7

Daphné Hong was born in Paris and illustrates children's books. At present she is working for the Illumination Mac Guff animation studio.

Her other passions are classical dance and traveling—both sources of inspiration that feed through to her everyday work. Her main failing is impatience and her best quality is curiosity.

daphne-h.blogspot.fr

Article 8

Carlos Felipe León was born in Bogotá, Colombia in 1981. After studying industrial engineering, he decided to come to France to pursue his passion for art. Graduating from Supinfocom in 2007, he works in animated movies, with a particular interest in visual development, color design, lighting, and artistic direction.

After working with many studios in Europe (Framestore, Illumination Entertainment, Neomis Animation, Bibo Films, etc.), he moved to San Francisco, where he now works for DreamWorks Animation. He also works as an illustrator (Nexus, Oculus Story Studio, etc.) and is developing his own projects in oils.

carlos-leon.com
facebook.com/carlosleon.artist

Article 9

A young graduate from the Gobelins School of Visual Arts, **Sandrine Han Jin Kuang** has worked for the LAIKA Onyx Film, Prima Linea, and Marathon Animation studios and for the youth press.

sumi-pimpampoum.blogspot.fr

Article 10

Stéphane Kardos was born in Laon, in the Aisne region of France, in 1971.

He studied animation at ESAAT in Roubaix, then illustration at Strasbourg Decorative Arts School. He worked first for Disney in 1997 in Paris, then in London in 2001 before joining the Disney team of artists in Los Angeles in 2007, where he is currently artistic director.

Stéphane works with Pixar, Lucasfilm, and Disney Feature Animation on different projects, and last year published his first book for children, *Judy Hopps and the Missing Jumbo Pop*, with Disney Publishing. Stéphane lives in Los Angeles with his lovely Swedish wife and two sons, Magnus and Nils.

stefsketches.blogspot.fr

Article 11

Christophe Lautrette studied at the School of Applied Arts in Toulouse, then at the Gobelins School of Visual Arts in Paris. He has worked for Disney France and for Bibo Films and for twenty years has been employed by DreamWorks Animation in Los Angeles. He has contributed to a number of productions, including *The Prince of Egypt*, *Spirit: Stallion of the Cimarron*, *The Road to Eldorado*, *Sinbad*, *Shark Tale*, *Madagascar*, *Rise of the Guardians*, and *Kung Fu Panda*. He was artistic director of *Bee Movie* and production designer on *The Croods*, and is now working on *Croods 2*.

Christophe is also the creator of *Moonshine*, a collective publication involving a number of artists.

lautrette.blogspot.fr

141

Bibliography

Publications

—

Abécassis, Éliette, and **Bongrand**, Caroline, *Le Corset invisible* (2007), Paris, Le Livre de Poche, "Littérature & Documents" collection, 2008

Adler, Laure, and **Bollmann**, Stefan, *Les femmes qui lisent sont dangereuses*, Paris, Flammarion, "Histoire de l'art" collection, 2006

Aragon, Louis, "Poème de l'avenir," *Le Fou d'Elsa* (1963), Paris, Gallimard, "Poésie/Gallimard" collection, 2002

Ariosto, Ludovico, *Orlando Furioso* (1516)

Auclair, Marcelle, *L'Amour, notes et maximes*, Paris, Hachette, 1963

Autain, Clémentine, *Alter égaux. Invitation au féminisme*, Paris, Robert Laffont, 2001

Badinter, Élisabeth, *Le Conflit. La femme et la mère* (2010), Paris, Le Livre de Poche, "Littérature & Documents" collection, 2011

Bard, Christine, *Une histoire politique du pantalon*, Paris, Seuil, 2010

Beauvoir, Simone de, *The Second Sex* (1949)

Benhabib, Djemila, *Les Soldats d'Allah à l'assaut de l'Occident*, Montreal, VLB éditeur, 2011

Blum, Léon, *Du mariage* (1907), in *L'Œuvre de Léon Blum*, Paris, Albin Michel, 1962

Butler, Judith, *Gender Trouble. Feminism and the Subversion of Identity*, New York, Routledge, 1990.

Chollet, Mona, *Beauté fatale. Les nouveaux visages d'une aliénation féminine*, Paris, La Découverte, "Zones," 2012

Cohen, Albert, *Belle du Seigneur* (1968), Paris, Gallimard, "Folio" collection, 1998

Condorcet, Nicolas de, *Cinq Mémoires sur l'instruction publique* (1791), Paris, Flammarion, "GF Philosophie" collection, 1993

Cusk, Rachel, *Arlington Park*, Faber, 2006

Davis, Angela, *Are Prisons Obsolete?* Seven Stories Press, 2003

Dawkins, Richard, *The God Delusion* (2006), Bantam, 2008

Denard, C. Carolyn (ed.), *Toni Morrison: Conversations*, Jackson, University Press of Mississippi, 2008

Despentes, Virginie, *King Kong Théorie* (2006), Paris, Le Livre de Poche, "Littérature & Documents" collection, 2007

Djavann, Chahdortt, *Bas les voiles!*, Paris, Gallimard, 2003

Engels, Friedrich, *The Origin of the Family, Private Property and the State*, (based on notes by Karl Marx, 1884)

Follett, Ken, *The Pillars of the Earth* (1989)

Fourier, Charles, *Vers la liberté en amour* (1817–1819), Paris, Gallimard, "Folio essais" collection, 1993

Fraisse, Geneviève, *La Fabrique du féminisme. Textes et entretiens*, Lyon, Le Passager clandestin, "Essais" collection, 2012

Fuller, Margaret, *Woman in the Nineteenth Century*, The Dial Magazine, 1843

Gandhi, Mahatma, *All Men Are Brothers* (1942–1956), Paris, UNESCO, 1958

Giroud, Françoise, *Si je mens*, Paris, Stock, 1972

Gournay, Marie de, *Égalité des hommes et des femmes* (1622), followed by Grief des dames, Paris, Arléa, 2008

Groult, Benoîte, *Ainsi soit-elle* (1975), Paris, Le Livre de Poche, "Littérature & Documents" collection, 1977
Le Féminisme au masculin (1977), Paris, Le Livre de Poche, "Littérature & Documents" collection, 2011
Histoire d'une évasion, Paris, Grasset, 1997

Henry, Natacha, *Les Mecs lourds ou le Paternalisme lubrique*, Paris, Robert Laffont, 2003

Héritier, Françoise, *Masculin/Féminin II. Dissoudre la hiérarchie*, Paris, Odile Jacob, 2008

Hugo, Victor, "Sur la tombe de Louise Julien, discours au cimetière Saint-Jean" (Jersey, July 26, 1853), *Actes et paroles. Pendant l'exil* (1875), Paris, Tredition, 2012
Choses vues (1860), Paris, Le Livre de Poche, "Les Classiques de Poche," 2013
"Lettre à Léon Richer" (June 8, 1872), *Écrits politiques*, anthology selected and annotated by Franck Laurent, Paris, Le Livre de poche, 2001

Khadra, Yasmina, *Ce que le jour doit à la nuit*, Paris, Julliard, 2008

Kristeva, Julia, *Colette. Un génie féminin*, Éditions de l'Aube, 2007

Leclerc, Annie, *Parole de femme* (1974), Arles, Actes Sud, "Babel" collection, 1974.

Michel, Louise, *Mémoires de Louise Michel écrits par elle-même* (1886), Paris, Hachette Livre BNF, 2012

Mill, John Stuart, *The Subjection of Women* (1869), London

Montesquieu, *Lettres persanes* (1721), Paris, Le Livre de Poche, "Classiques", 2006

Morrison, Toni, *A Mercy*, Knopf, 2008

Nasreen, Taslima, *Femmes, manifestez-vous!* (writings gathered from 1989 and 1990), Paris, Éditions des femmes, 1994

Oldenbourg, Zoé, *La Pierre angulaire* (1953), Paris, Gallimard, "Folio" collection, 1972

Onfray, Michel, *Traité d'athéologie*, Paris, Grasset, 2005

Pelletier, Madeleine, *L'Émancipation sexuelle de la femme* (1911), Paris, Hachette Livre BNF, "Sciences sociales" collection, 2016

Perrot, Michelle, *Les Femmes ou les Silences de l'histoire* (1998), Paris, Flammarion, "Champs histoire" collection, 2012

Richer, Léon, *La Femme libre*, E. Dentu, 1877

Rimbaud, Arthur, letter to Paul Demeny (Charleville, May 15, 1871), in *Œuvres complètes*, Paris, Flammarion, "GF" collection, 2016

Saint-Just, Louis Antoine de, *L'Esprit de la Révolution et de la constitution de France* (1791), in *Œuvres complètes*, Paris, Gallimard, "Folio histoire" collection, 2004

Sand, George, "Lettre à l'abbé de Lamennais" (Nohant, February 28, 1837), in *Correspondance. Volume III: July 1835–April 1837*, Paris, Classiques Garnier, 2013

"Sixième lettre à Marcie" (*Le Monde*, March 27, 1837), in *Lettres à Marcie, Perpignan*, Paléo, 2014

Shakespeare, William, *As You Like It* (1599)

Stendhal, *Rome, Naples et Florence* (1826), Paris, Gallimard, "Folio Classique" collection, 1987

Sullivan, J. Courtney, *Commencement*, Knopf, 2009

Tinayre, Marcelle, *La Veillée des armes* (1915), Paris, Éditions des femmes, 2015

Tristan, Flora, *Pérégrinations d'une paria* (1833–1834), Paris, Hachette Livre BNF, "Sciences sociales" collection, 2016

Wolf, Naomi, *The Beauty Myth: How Images of Beauty Are Used Against Women* (1990), Needs English reference.

Wollstonecraft, Mary, *A Vindication of the Rights of Woman* (1792)

Woolf, Virginia, *A Room of One's Own* (1929)

Articles and speeches

—

Auclert, Hubertine, speech given at the 3rd Socialist Workers' Congress, Marseille, October 22, 1879; available on the Alternative libertaire website [alternativelibertaire.org]

Chaumont, Louise de, "La Marseillaise des cotillons," *La République des femmes, journal des cotillons*, #1, June 1848

Clinton, Hillary, speech given at the UN 4th World Conference on Women, Beijing, September 5, 1995

Speech given at the National Building Museum, Washington, June 7, 2008

David-Néel, Alexandra, "Les femmes et la question sociale," *La Fronde*, May 28, 1902

Deraismes, Maria, "Ce que veulent les femmes," *Le Droit des femmes*, #1 (April 10, 1869); reproduced in *Ce que veulent les femmes. Articles et discours de 1869 à 1894*, Paris, Syros, 1980

Durand, Marguerite, *Notes de conférence sur le vote des femmes* (undated), manuscript, Marguerite Durand Library, Paris

Féministes laïques algériennes et iraniennes (collectif), "Lettre ouverte à nos amies féministes," 2009

Goldman, Emma, text of a lecture published in *Mother Earth* (#1, March 1906), also published in *La Tragédie de l'émancipation féminine* (1906), Paris, Syros, 1980

Jong, Erica, "Entretien avec Sophie Lannes," July–August 1978

"Lip au féminin," *Les Pétroleuses* (#0, 1974); available on the *Fragments d'histoire de la gauche radicale* website. Archives and sources of the radical and/or extraparliamentary left [archivesautonomies.org]

Kollontaï, Alexandra, "Les problèmes de la prostitution", *La Bataille socialiste*, 1909

Loiseau, Jeanne, aka Daniel-Lesueur, "L'Évolution féminine, ses résultats Économiques," speech given at the International Congress of Trade and Industry, Universal Exhibition, 1900

Pankhurst, Emmeline, quoted in *Human Development Report*, United Nations Development Program (UNDP), 2013

Peillon, Vincent, and **Vallaud-Belkacem**, Najat, "Pour plus d'égalité entre filles et garçons à l'école," *Le Monde*, September 25, 2012

"Pourquoi je suis au mouvement de libération des femmes," *Le Torchon brûle*, #0, published as an insert in the first issue of *L'Idiot Liberté*, December 1970

Roudy, Yvette, "La parité domestiquée," *Le Monde*, September 5, 2004

Roussel, Nelly, speech given at a demonstration in support of paternity searches, February 9, 1910

Touraine, Marisol, press release, International Day for the Elimination of Violence against Women, November 25, 2015

Veil, Simone, address to the French National Assembly on reasons for reforming abortion legislation (November 26, 1974), published in *Les hommes aussi s'en souviennent*, Paris, Stock, 2004

Whitton, Charlotte, in *Canada Month*, June 1963.

An Hachette UK Company
www.hachette.co.uy

First published in Great Britain in 2018 by
ILEX, a division of Octopus Publishing Group Ltd.

Octopus Publishing Group
Carmelite House, 50 Victoria Embankment
London, EC4Y 0DZ

Distributed in the US by
Hachette Book Group
1290 Avenue of the Americas, 4th and 5th Floors
New York, NY 10104

Distributed in Canada by
Canadian Manda Group
664 Annette St., Toronto, Ontario
Canada M6S 2C8

Publisher: **Roly Allen**
Editorial Director: **Helen Rochester**
Managing Editor: **Frank Gallaugher**
Senior Editor: **Rachel Silverlight**
Admin Assistant: **Stephanie Hetherington**
Art Director: **Julie Weir**
Production Controller: **Meskerem Berhane**

Introductions on pages 6–7 and 82–83
written by Roly Allen

Produced by Éditions du Chêne
58, rue Jean Bleuzen
92178 Vanves Cedex

© 2017, Hachette Livre – Éditions du Chêne
www.editionsduchene.fr

Managing director: **Fabienne Kriegel**
Editor-in-chief: **Fanny Delahaye**
Editorial coordinator: **Léa Delourme**
Artistic direction: **Sabine Houplain**
Layout: **Les PAOistes**
Cover: **Claire-Lise Bengue**
Text selection: **Dominique Foufelle**
Translation from French: **Alayne Pullen**,
in association with **First Edition Translations Ltd,
Cambridge, UK**
Proofreading and correction: **Valérie Mettais**
Fabrication: **Nicole Thiériot-Pichon**
Photoengraving: **Quat'coul**
Partnerships and direct sales:
Mathilde Barrois (mbarrois@hachette-livre.fr)
Press officer:
Hélène Maurice (hmaurice@hachette-livre.fr)

Acknowledgments

The publishers would like to thank most
warmly all the artists who contributed to this
book. Without their generosity, talent, and
enthusiasm this wonderful project would not
have been possible.

ISBN 978-1-78157-567-3

A CIP catalog record for this book is available from
the British Library.

Printed in China

10 9 8 7 6 5 4 3 2 1